MW01129888

Individual Studies for Grade 4

A Year of Lesson Plans
for Language Arts, Math, and Science

by
Sonya Shafer

Individual Studies for Grade 4: A Year of Lesson Plans for Language Arts, Math, and Science
© 2015, Sonya Shafer

All rights reserved. However, we grant permission to make printed copies or use this work on multiple electronic devices for members of your immediate household. Quantity discounts are available for classroom and co-op use. Please contact us for details.

Cover Design: John Shafer and Sarah Shafer

ISBN 978-1-61634-312-5 printed
ISBN 978-1-61634-313-2 electronic download

Published by
Simply Charlotte Mason, LLC
930 New Hope Road #11-892
Lawrenceville, Georgia 30045
simplycharlottemason.com

Printed by PrintLogic, Inc.
Monroe, Georgia, USA

Contents

How to Use

Most school subjects can be taught to your whole family together, but some subjects are best taught individually so you can progress at the student's pace. This book of lesson plans contains suggestions and assignments for individual work for students in grade 4. Complete one lesson plan per day to finish these studies in a school year.

The lesson plans in this book cover language arts, science, and math.

Language Arts

Students will progress in spelling, capitalization, punctuation, and English usage guidelines using the literary passages presented in *Spelling Wisdom, Book 1,* and the guided discovery lessons in *Using Language Well, Book 1.* The first half of these books was covered in grade 3, the rest will be completed this year.

Written narration will be introduced to encourage your student to begin capturing his thoughts on paper and applying guidelines he has learned about English usage and mechanics. Rubrics and further instructions are provided in the *Using Language Well, Book 1, Teacher Guide and Answer Key* to help with this process.

Science

Science can be done individually, or if you have more than one student in grades 1–6, they may all do one science course together. Simply Charlotte Mason has several to choose from.

Nature Study is an important part of science studies; be sure to include it. Follow the Nature Study suggestions in your selected science course or use the nature notebook, *Journaling a Year in Nature,* to guide your weekly study. Nature Study can be done all together as a family, but we have included reminders in these individual plans too.

Math

Use the math curriculum of your choice. These lesson plans will include reminders to work on it. As with other individual work, be sure to go at your student's pace.

Complete Year's Resources List

- *Spelling Wisdom, Book 1*
  Students will complete the last half of this book this year; the first half was covered in grade 3.
- *Using Language Well, Book 1, Student Book*
  Students will complete the last half of the student book this year; the first half was covered in grade 3.
- *Using Language Well, Book 1, Teacher Guide and Answer Key*
- Simply Charlotte Mason science course of choice
- *Journaling a Year in Nature* notebooks, one per person (optional)
- Math course of choice
- Typing course of choice

Note: All resources except math and typing are available from Simply Charlotte Mason.

Term 1

(12 weeks; 5 lessons/week)

Term 1 Resources List

- ~~*Spelling Wisdom, Book 1*~~ Wordly wise
- ~~*Using Language Well, Book 1, Student Book*~~
- ~~*Using Language Well, Book 1, Teacher Guide and Answer Key*~~ language lessons for living education
- Simply Charlotte Mason (SCM) science course of choice
- *Journaling a Year in Nature* notebooks (optional)
- ~~Typing course of choice~~
- Math course of choice Saxon

Weekly Schedule

Day One	Day Two	Day Three	Day Four	Day Five
Math (20–30 min.)	Math (20–30 min.)	Math (20–30 min.)	Math (20–30 min.)	Math (20–30 min.)
	Science (20 min.)		Science (20 min.)	(Nature Study)
Spelling Wisdom & Using Language Well (15 min.)	Typing (10–15 min.)	Spelling Wisdom & Using Language Well (15 min.)		Typing (10–15 min.)

Lesson 1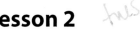

Materials Needed
- Math course of choice
- *Spelling Wisdom, Book 1*
- *Using Language Well, Book 1, Student Book*
- *Using Language Well, Book 1, Teacher Guide and Answer Key*

Math: Work on your selected math curriculum for about 30 minutes.

Spelling and English: Complete *Using Language Well, Book 1,* Lesson 71.

Tip: Most of the lessons assigned in Using Language Well, Book 1, *for grade 4 are designed to be completed independently. Check your student's work and oversee the dictation portion when he is ready. See the* Using Language Well, Book 1, Teacher Guide and Answer Key *for details.*

Lesson 2

Materials Needed
- Math course of choice
- SCM science course of choice
- Typing course of choice

Math: Work on your selected math curriculum for about 30 minutes.

Science: In your SCM science course, complete the first assignment for Week 1.

Typing: Work on your selected typing course for about 15 minutes.

Lesson 3

Materials Needed
- Math course of choice
- *Spelling Wisdom, Book 1*
- *Using Language Well, Book 1, Student Book*
- *Using Language Well, Book 1, Teacher Guide and Answer Key*

Math: Work on your selected math curriculum for about 30 minutes.

Spelling and English: Complete *Using Language Well, Book 1,* Lesson 72.

Lesson 4

Materials Needed
- SCM science course of choice

Notes

• Math course of choice

Science: In your SCM science course, complete the second assignment for Week 1.

Math: Work on your selected math curriculum for about 30 minutes.

Tip: You may complete school assignments in any order that works best for your family's schedule. Try to sequence lessons throughout the day to use different parts of the student's brain and body as you go along. In other words, don't schedule two "book-heavy" assignments back to back. Put the math assignment in between or do some Family work—such as Picture Study or Music Study—in between to break up the readings. Each lesson plan in this book is sequenced to help you with that important principle.

Lesson 5

Materials Needed
• Math course of choice
• Typing course of choice
• *Journaling a Year in Nature* notebooks (optional)

Math: Work on your selected math curriculum for about 30 minutes.

Typing: Work on your selected typing course for about 15 minutes.

Nature Study: Take the whole family outside for nature study.

Tip: Follow the Nature Study suggestions in your SCM science course or use the nature notebook, Journaling a Year in Nature, *to guide your weekly study.*

Lesson 6

Materials Needed
• Math course of choice
• *Spelling Wisdom, Book 1*
• *Using Language Well, Book 1, Student Book*
• *Using Language Well, Book 1, Teacher Guide and Answer Key*

Math: Work on your selected math curriculum for about 30 minutes.

Spelling and English: Complete *Using Language Well, Book 1,* Lesson 73.

> *Reminder: If your child is fluent in oral narrations from his history, geography, Bible, or science readings, ask him to write one of his narrations each week. Continue oral narrations daily.*

Lesson 7 ~ Tues

Materials Needed
- Math course of choice
- SCM science course of choice
- Typing course of choice

Math: Work on your selected math curriculum for about 30 minutes.

Science: In your SCM science course, complete the first assignment for Week 2.

Typing: Work on your selected typing course for about 15 minutes.

Lesson 8 ~ Wed

Materials Needed
- Math course of choice
- *Spelling Wisdom, Book 1*
- *Using Language Well, Book 1, Student Book*
- *Using Language Well, Book 1, Teacher Guide and Answer Key*

Math: Work on your selected math curriculum for about 30 minutes.

Spelling and English: Complete *Using Language Well, Book 1,* Lesson 74.

Lesson 9 ~ Thur

Materials Needed
- SCM science course of choice
- Math course of choice

Science: In your SCM science course, complete the second assignment for Week 2.

Math: Work on your selected math curriculum for about 30 minutes.

Lesson 10 ~ Friday

Materials Needed
- Math course of choice
- Typing course of choice
- *Journaling a Year in Nature* notebooks (optional)

Math: Work on your selected math curriculum for about 30 minutes.

Typing: Work on your selected typing course for about 15 minutes.

Nature Study: Take the whole family outside for nature study.

Tip: Follow the Nature Study suggestions in your SCM science course or use the nature notebook, Journaling a Year in Nature, *to guide your weekly study.*

Lesson 11

Materials Needed
- Math course of choice
- *Spelling Wisdom, Book 1*
- *Using Language Well, Book 1, Student Book*
- *Using Language Well, Book 1, Teacher Guide and Answer Key*

Math: Work on your selected math curriculum for about 30 minutes.

Spelling and English: Complete *Using Language Well, Book 1,* Lesson 75.

Reminder: Assign your student to write one of his narrations from his history, geography, Bible, or science readings this week. Continue oral narrations daily.

Lesson 12

Materials Needed
- Math course of choice
- SCM science course of choice
- Typing course of choice

Math: Work on your selected math curriculum for about 30 minutes.

Science: In your SCM science course, complete the first assignment for Week 3.

Typing: Work on your selected typing course for about 15 minutes.

Lesson 13

Materials Needed
- Math course of choice
- *Spelling Wisdom, Book 1*
- *Using Language Well, Book 1, Student Book*

- *Using Language Well, Book 1, Teacher Guide and Answer Key*

Math: Work on your selected math curriculum for about 30 minutes.

Spelling and English: Complete *Using Language Well, Book 1,* Lesson 76.

Lesson 14   Th

Materials Needed
- SCM science course of choice
- Math course of choice

Science: In your SCM science course, complete the second assignment for Week 3.

Math: Work on your selected math curriculum for about 30 minutes.

Tip: If your student would like to, encourage him to start a Book of Mottoes, or a commonplace book,—a journal in which he records personally selected quotations, poetry, excerpts, or Scripture passages that are meaningful to him. You might allow him to purchase a special journal for this ongoing project. You will see periodic reminders in these lesson plans; mention them only if your student is interested.

Lesson 15   F

Materials Needed
- Math course of choice
- Typing course of choice
- *Journaling a Year in Nature* notebooks (optional)

Math: Work on your selected math curriculum for about 30 minutes.

Typing: Work on your selected typing course for about 15 minutes.

Nature Study: Take the whole family outside for nature study.

Tip: Follow the Nature Study suggestions in your SCM science course or use the nature notebook, Journaling a Year in Nature, *to guide your weekly study.*

Lesson 16   M

Materials Needed
- Math course of choice

Notes

- *Spelling Wisdom, Book 1*
- *Using Language Well, Book 1, Student Book*
- *Using Language Well, Book 1, Teacher Guide and Answer Key*

Math: Work on your selected math curriculum for about 30 minutes.

Spelling and English: Complete *Using Language Well, Book 1,* Lesson 77.

Reminder: Assign your student to write one of his narrations from his history, geography, Bible, or science readings this week. Continue oral narrations daily.

Lesson 17

Materials Needed
- Math course of choice
- SCM science course of choice
- Typing course of choice

Math: Work on your selected math curriculum for about 30 minutes.

Science: In your SCM science course, complete the first assignment for Week 4.

Typing: Work on your selected typing course for about 15 minutes.

Lesson 18

Materials Needed
- Math course of choice
- *Spelling Wisdom, Book 1*
- *Using Language Well, Book 1, Student Book*
- *Using Language Well, Book 1, Teacher Guide and Answer Key*

Math: Work on your selected math curriculum for about 30 minutes.

Spelling and English: Complete *Using Language Well, Book 1,* Lesson 78.

Lesson 19 Th

Materials Needed
- SCM science course of choice
- Math course of choice

Science: In your SCM science course, complete the second assignment for Week 4.

Math: Work on your selected math curriculum for about 30 minutes.

Lesson 20

Materials Needed
- Math course of choice
- Typing course of choice
- *Journaling a Year in Nature* notebooks (optional)

Math: Work on your selected math curriculum for about 30 minutes.

Typing: Work on your selected typing course for about 15 minutes.

Nature Study: Take the whole family outside for nature study.

Lesson 21 M 9/23

Materials Needed
- Math course of choice
- *Spelling Wisdom, Book 1*
- *Using Language Well, Book 1, Student Book*
- *Using Language Well, Book 1, Teacher Guide and Answer Key*

Math: Work on your selected math curriculum for about 30 minutes.

Spelling and English: Complete *Using Language Well, Book 1*, Lesson 79.

Reminder: Assign your student to write one of his narrations from his history, geography, Bible, or science readings this week. Continue oral narrations daily.

Lesson 22 T

Materials Needed
- Math course of choice
- SCM science course of choice
- Typing course of choice

Math: Work on your selected math curriculum for about 30 minutes.

Science: In your SCM science course, complete the first assignment for Week 5.

Typing: Work on your selected typing course for about 15 minutes.

Lesson 23 W

Materials Needed
- Math course of choice

- *Spelling Wisdom, Book 1*
- *Using Language Well, Book 1, Student Book*
- *Using Language Well, Book 1, Teacher Guide and Answer Key*

Math: Work on your selected math curriculum for about 30 minutes.

Spelling and English: Complete *Using Language Well, Book 1,* Lesson 80.

Lesson 24 Th

Materials Needed
- SCM science course of choice
- Math course of choice

Science: In your SCM science course, complete the second assignment for Week 5.

Math: Work on your selected math curriculum for about 30 minutes.

Lesson 25 F

Materials Needed
- Math course of choice
- Typing course of choice
- *Journaling a Year in Nature* notebooks (optional)

Math: Work on your selected math curriculum for about 30 minutes.

Typing: Work on your selected typing course for about 15 minutes.

Nature Study: Take the whole family outside for nature study.

Lesson 26

Materials Needed
- Math course of choice
- *Spelling Wisdom, Book 1*
- *Using Language Well, Book 1, Student Book*
- *Using Language Well, Book 1, Teacher Guide and Answer Key*

Math: Work on your selected math curriculum for about 30 minutes.

Spelling and English: Complete *Using Language Well, Book 1,* Lesson 81.

_____

Reminder: Assign your student to write one of his narrations from his history, geography, Bible, or science readings this week. Continue oral narrations daily.

_____

Lesson 27

Materials Needed
- Math course of choice
- SCM science course of choice
- Typing course of choice

Math: Work on your selected math curriculum for about 30 minutes.

Science: In your SCM science course, complete the first assignment for Week 6.

Typing: Work on your selected typing course for about 15 minutes.

Lesson 28

Materials Needed
- Math course of choice
- *Spelling Wisdom, Book 1*
- *Using Language Well, Book 1, Student Book*
- *Using Language Well, Book 1, Teacher Guide and Answer Key*

Math: Work on your selected math curriculum for about 30 minutes.

Spelling and English: Complete *Using Language Well, Book 1,* Lesson 82.

Lesson 29

Materials Needed
- SCM science course of choice
- Math course of choice

Science: In your SCM science course, complete the second assignment for Week 6.

Math: Work on your selected math curriculum for about 30 minutes.

Tip: Remind your student to record in his Book of Mottoes any meaningful quotations, poetry, excerpts, or Scripture passages from recent readings (if he is interested in that ongoing project).

Lesson 30

Materials Needed
- Math course of choice
- Typing course of choice
- *Journaling a Year in Nature* notebooks (optional)

Notes

Math: Work on your selected math curriculum for about 30 minutes.

Typing: Work on your selected typing course for about 15 minutes.

Nature Study: Take the whole family outside for nature study.

Lesson 31

Materials Needed
- Math course of choice
- *Spelling Wisdom, Book 1*
- *Using Language Well, Book 1, Student Book*
- *Using Language Well, Book 1, Teacher Guide and Answer Key*

Math: Work on your selected math curriculum for about 30 minutes.

Spelling and English: Complete *Using Language Well, Book 1,* Lesson 83.

Reminder: Assign your student to write one narration from his history, geography, Bible, or science readings this week. Use Rubric 1.1 from Using Language Well, Book 1, Teacher Guide and Answer Key *to help you evaluate his writing. Continue oral narrations daily.*

Lesson 32

Materials Needed
- Math course of choice
- SCM science course of choice
- Typing course of choice

Math: Work on your selected math curriculum for about 30 minutes.

Science: In your SCM science course, complete the first assignment for Week 7.

Typing: Work on your selected typing course for about 15 minutes.

Lesson 33

Materials Needed
- Math course of choice
- *Spelling Wisdom, Book 1*
- *Using Language Well, Book 1, Student Book*
- *Using Language Well, Book 1, Teacher Guide and Answer Key*

Math: Work on your selected math curriculum for about 30 minutes.

Spelling and English: Complete *Using Language Well, Book 1,* Lesson 84.

Lesson 34   *Th.*

Materials Needed
- SCM science course of choice
- Math course of choice

Science: In your SCM science course, complete the second assignment for Week 7.

Math: Work on your selected math curriculum for about 30 minutes.

Lesson 35   *F*

Materials Needed
- Math course of choice
- Typing course of choice
- *Journaling a Year in Nature* notebooks (optional)

Math: Work on your selected math curriculum for about 30 minutes.

Typing: Work on your selected typing course for about 15 minutes.

Nature Study: Take the whole family outside for nature study.

Lesson 36   *M*

Materials Needed
- Math course of choice
- *Spelling Wisdom, Book 1*
- *Using Language Well, Book 1, Student Book*
- *Using Language Well, Book 1, Teacher Guide and Answer Key*

Math: Work on your selected math curriculum for about 30 minutes.

Spelling and English: Complete *Using Language Well, Book 1*, Lesson 85.

Reminder: Assign your student to write one narration from his history, geography, Bible, or science readings this week. Use Rubric 1.1 from Using Language Well, Book 1, Teacher Guide and Answer Key *to help you evaluate his writing. Continue oral narrations daily.*

Lesson 37   *T*

Materials Needed
- Math course of choice
- SCM science course of choice

- Typing course of choice

Math: Work on your selected math curriculum for about 30 minutes.

Science: In your SCM science course, complete the first assignment for Week 8.

Typing: Work on your selected typing course for about 15 minutes.

Lesson 38 W

Materials Needed
- Math course of choice
- *Spelling Wisdom, Book 1*
- *Using Language Well, Book 1, Student Book*
- *Using Language Well, Book 1, Teacher Guide and Answer Key*

Math: Work on your selected math curriculum for about 30 minutes.

Spelling and English: Complete *Using Language Well, Book 1,* Lesson 86.

Lesson 39 Th

Materials Needed
- SCM science course of choice
- Math course of choice

Science: In your SCM science course, complete the second assignment for Week 8.

Math: Work on your selected math curriculum for about 30 minutes.

Lesson 40 F

Materials Needed
- Math course of choice
- Typing course of choice
- *Journaling a Year in Nature* notebooks (optional)

Math: Work on your selected math curriculum for about 30 minutes.

Typing: Work on your selected typing course for about 15 minutes.

Nature Study: Take the whole family outside for nature study.

Lesson 41

Materials Needed
- Math course of choice

- *Spelling Wisdom, Book 1*
- *Using Language Well, Book 1, Student Book*
- *Using Language Well, Book 1, Teacher Guide and Answer Key*

Math: Work on your selected math curriculum for about 30 minutes.

Spelling and English: Complete *Using Language Well, Book 1,* Lesson 87.

Reminder: Assign your student to write one narration from his history, geography, Bible, or science readings this week. Use Rubric 1.1 from Using Language Well, Book 1, Teacher Guide and Answer Key *to help you evaluate his writing. Continue oral narrations daily.*

Lesson 42

Materials Needed
- Math course of choice
- SCM science course of choice
- Typing course of choice

Math: Work on your selected math curriculum for about 30 minutes.

Science: In your SCM science course, complete the first assignment for Week 9.

Typing: Work on your selected typing course for about 15 minutes.

Lesson 43

Materials Needed
- Math course of choice
- *Spelling Wisdom, Book 1*
- *Using Language Well, Book 1, Student Book*
- *Using Language Well, Book 1, Teacher Guide and Answer Key*

Math: Work on your selected math curriculum for about 30 minutes.

Spelling and English: Complete *Using Language Well, Book 1,* Lesson 88.

Lesson 44

Materials Needed
- SCM science course of choice
- Math course of choice

Science: In your SCM science course, complete the second assignment for Week 9.

Math: Work on your selected math curriculum for about 30 minutes.

Tip: Remind your student to record in his Book of Mottoes any meaningful quotations, poetry, excerpts, or Scripture passages from recent readings (if he is interested in that ongoing project).

Lesson 45

Materials Needed
- Math course of choice
- Typing course of choice
- *Journaling a Year in Nature* notebooks (optional)

Math: Work on your selected math curriculum for about 30 minutes.

Typing: Work on your selected typing course for about 15 minutes.

Nature Study: Take the whole family outside for nature study.

Lesson 46

Materials Needed
- Math course of choice
- *Spelling Wisdom, Book 1*
- *Using Language Well, Book 1, Student Book*
- *Using Language Well, Book 1, Teacher Guide and Answer Key*

Math: Work on your selected math curriculum for about 30 minutes.

Spelling and English: Complete *Using Language Well, Book 1,* Lesson 89.

Reminder: Assign your student to write one narration from his history, geography, Bible, or science readings this week. Use Rubric 1.1 from Using Language Well, Book 1, Teacher Guide and Answer Key *to help you evaluate his writing. Continue oral narrations daily.*

Lesson 47

Materials Needed
- Math course of choice
- SCM science course of choice
- Typing course of choice

Math: Work on your selected math curriculum for about 30 minutes.

Science: In your SCM science course, complete the first assignment for Week 10.

Typing: Work on your selected typing course for about 15 minutes.

Lesson 48

Materials Needed
- Math course of choice
- *Spelling Wisdom, Book 1*
- *Using Language Well, Book 1, Student Book*
- *Using Language Well, Book 1, Teacher Guide and Answer Key*

Math: Work on your selected math curriculum for about 30 minutes.

Spelling and English: Complete *Using Language Well, Book 1,* Lesson 90.

Lesson 49

Materials Needed
- SCM science course of choice
- Math course of choice

Science: In your SCM science course, complete the second assignment for Week 10.

Math: Work on your selected math curriculum for about 30 minutes.

Lesson 50

Materials Needed
- Math course of choice
- Typing course of choice
- *Journaling a Year in Nature* notebooks (optional)

Math: Work on your selected math curriculum for about 30 minutes.

Typing: Work on your selected typing course for about 15 minutes.

Nature Study: Take the whole family outside for nature study.

Lesson 51

Materials Needed
- Math course of choice
- *Spelling Wisdom, Book 1*
- *Using Language Well, Book 1, Student Book*
- *Using Language Well, Book 1, Teacher Guide and Answer Key*

Math: Work on your selected math curriculum for about 30 minutes.

Spelling and English: Complete *Using Language Well, Book 1,* Lesson 91.

Reminder: Assign your student to write one narration from his history, geography, Bible, or science readings this week. Use Rubric 1.1 from Using Language Well, Book 1, Teacher Guide and Answer Key *to help you evaluate his writing. Continue oral narrations daily.*

Lesson 52

Materials Needed
- Math course of choice
- SCM science course of choice
- Typing course of choice

Math: Work on your selected math curriculum for about 30 minutes.

Science: In your SCM science course, complete the first assignment for Week 11.

Typing: Work on your selected typing course for about 15 minutes.

Lesson 53

Materials Needed
- Math course of choice
- *Spelling Wisdom, Book 1*
- *Using Language Well, Book 1, Student Book*
- *Using Language Well, Book 1, Teacher Guide and Answer Key*

Math: Work on your selected math curriculum for about 30 minutes.

Spelling and English: Complete *Using Language Well, Book 1,* Lesson 92.

Lesson 54

Materials Needed
- SCM science course of choice
- Math course of choice

Science: In your SCM science course, complete the second assignment for Week 11.

Math: Work on your selected math curriculum for about 30 minutes.

Lesson 55

Materials Needed
- Math course of choice
- Typing course of choice
- *Journaling a Year in Nature* notebooks (optional)

Math: Work on your selected math curriculum for about 30 minutes.

Typing: Work on your selected typing course for about 15 minutes.

Nature Study: Take the whole family outside for nature study.

Lesson 56

Materials Needed
- Math course of choice
- *Spelling Wisdom, Book 1*
- *Using Language Well, Book 1, Student Book*
- *Using Language Well, Book 1, Teacher Guide and Answer Key*

Math: Work on your selected math curriculum for about 30 minutes.

Spelling and English: Complete *Using Language Well, Book 1,* Lesson 93.

Reminder: Assign your student to write one narration from his history, geography, Bible, or science readings this week. Begin using Rubric 1.2 from Using Language Well, Book 1, Teacher Guide and Answer Key *to help you evaluate his writing. Continue oral narrations daily.*

Lesson 57

Materials Needed
- Math course of choice
- SCM science course of choice
- Typing course of choice

Math: Work on your selected math curriculum for about 30 minutes.

Science: In your SCM science course, complete the first assignment for Week 12.

Typing: Work on your selected typing course for about 15 minutes.

Lesson 58

Materials Needed
- Math course of choice
- *Spelling Wisdom, Book 1*
- *Using Language Well, Book 1, Student Book*
- *Using Language Well, Book 1, Teacher Guide and Answer Key*

Math: Work on your selected math curriculum for about 30 minutes.

Spelling and English: Complete *Using Language Well, Book 1,* Lesson 94.

Lesson 59

Materials Needed
- SCM science course of choice
- Math course of choice

Science: In your SCM science course, complete the second assignment for Week 12.

Math: Work on your selected math curriculum for about 30 minutes.

Tip: Remind your student to record in his Book of Mottoes any meaningful quotations, poetry, excerpts, or Scripture passages from recent readings (if he is interested in that ongoing project).

Lesson 60

Materials Needed
- Math course of choice
- Typing course of choice
- *Journaling a Year in Nature* notebooks (optional)

Math: Work on your selected math curriculum for about 30 minutes.

Typing: Work on your selected typing course for about 15 minutes.

Nature Study: Take the whole family outside for nature study.

Term 2

(12 weeks; 5 lessons/week)

Term 2 Resources List

- *Spelling Wisdom, Book 1*
- *Using Language Well, Book 1, Student Book*
- *Using Language Well, Book 1, Teacher Guide and Answer Key*
- Simply Charlotte Mason (SCM) science course of choice
- *Journaling a Year in Nature* notebooks (optional)
- Typing course of choice
- Math course of choice

Weekly Schedule

Day One	Day Two	Day Three	Day Four	Day Five
Math (20–30 min.)	Math (20–30 min.)	Math (20–30 min.)	Math (20–30 min.)	Math (20–30 min.)
(Nature Study)		Science (20 min.)		Science (20 min.)
Typing (10–15 min.)	Spelling Wisdom & Using Language Well (15 min.)		Spelling Wisdom & Using Language Well (15 min.)	Typing (10–15 min.)

Lesson 61

Materials Needed
- Math course of choice
- Typing course of choice
- *Journaling a Year in Nature* notebooks (optional)

Math: Work on your selected math curriculum for about 30 minutes.

Typing: Work on your selected typing course for about 15 minutes.

Nature Study: Take the whole family outside for nature study.

Lesson 62

Materials Needed
- Math course of choice
- *Spelling Wisdom, Book 1*
- *Using Language Well, Book 1, Student Book*
- *Using Language Well, Book 1, Teacher Guide and Answer Key*

Math: Work on your selected math curriculum for about 30 minutes.

Spelling and English: Complete *Using Language Well, Book 1,* Lesson 95.

Reminder: Assign your student to write one narration from his history, geography, Bible, or science readings this week. Use Rubric 1.2 from Using Language Well, Book 1, Teacher Guide and Answer Key *to help you evaluate his writing. Continue oral narrations daily.*

Lesson 63

Materials Needed
- SCM science course of choice
- Math course of choice

Science: In your SCM science course, complete the first assignment for Week 13.

Math: Work on your selected math curriculum for about 30 minutes.

Lesson 64

Materials Needed
- Math course of choice
- *Spelling Wisdom, Book 1*

Notes

- *Using Language Well, Book 1, Student Book*
- *Using Language Well, Book 1, Teacher Guide and Answer Key*

Math: Work on your selected math curriculum for about 30 minutes.

Spelling and English: Complete *Using Language Well, Book 1,* Lesson 96.

Lesson 65

Materials Needed
- Typing course of choice
- SCM science course of choice
- Math course of choice

Typing: Work on your selected typing course for about 15 minutes.

Science: In your SCM science course, complete the second assignment for Week 13.

Math: Work on your selected math curriculum for about 30 minutes.

Lesson 66

Materials Needed
- Math course of choice
- Typing course of choice
- *Journaling a Year in Nature* notebooks (optional)

Math: Work on your selected math curriculum for about 30 minutes.

Typing: Work on your selected typing course for about 15 minutes.

Nature Study: Take the whole family outside for nature study.

Lesson 67

Materials Needed
- Math course of choice
- *Spelling Wisdom, Book 1*
- *Using Language Well, Book 1, Student Book*
- *Using Language Well, Book 1, Teacher Guide and Answer Key*

Math: Work on your selected math curriculum for about 30 minutes.

Spelling and English: Complete *Using Language Well, Book 1,* Lesson 97.

Reminder: Assign your student to write one narration from his history, geography, Bible, or science readings this week. Use Rubric 1.2 from Using

Language Well, Book 1, Teacher Guide and Answer Key *to help you evaluate his writing. Continue oral narrations daily.*

Lesson 68

Materials Needed
- SCM science course of choice
- Math course of choice

Science: In your SCM science course, complete the first assignment for Week 14.

Math: Work on your selected math curriculum for about 30 minutes.

Lesson 69

Materials Needed
- Math course of choice
- *Spelling Wisdom, Book 1*
- *Using Language Well, Book 1, Student Book*
- *Using Language Well, Book 1, Teacher Guide and Answer Key*

Math: Work on your selected math curriculum for about 30 minutes.

Spelling and English: Complete *Using Language Well, Book 1,* Lesson 98.

Lesson 70

Materials Needed
- Typing course of choice
- SCM science course of choice
- Math course of choice

Typing: Work on your selected typing course for about 15 minutes.

Science: In your SCM science course, complete the second assignment for Week 14.

Math: Work on your selected math curriculum for about 30 minutes.

Lesson 71

Materials Needed
- Math course of choice
- Typing course of choice
- *Journaling a Year in Nature* notebooks (optional)

Math: Work on your selected math curriculum for about 30 minutes.

Typing: Work on your selected typing course for about 15 minutes.

Nature Study: Take the whole family outside for nature study.

Lesson 72

Materials Needed
- Math course of choice
- *Spelling Wisdom, Book 1*
- *Using Language Well, Book 1, Student Book*
- *Using Language Well, Book 1, Teacher Guide and Answer Key*

Math: Work on your selected math curriculum for about 30 minutes.

Spelling and English: Complete *Using Language Well, Book 1,* Lesson 99.

Reminder: Assign your student to write one narration from his history, geography, Bible, or science readings this week. Begin using Rubric 1.3 from Using Language Well, Book 1, Teacher Guide and Answer Key *to help you evaluate his writing. Continue oral narrations daily.*

Lesson 73

Materials Needed
- SCM science course of choice
- Math course of choice

Science: In your SCM science course, complete the first assignment for Week 15.

Math: Work on your selected math curriculum for about 30 minutes.

Tip: Remind your student to record in his Book of Mottoes any meaningful quotations, poetry, excerpts, or Scripture passages from recent readings (if he is interested in that ongoing project).

Lesson 74

Materials Needed
- Math course of choice
- *Spelling Wisdom, Book 1*
- *Using Language Well, Book 1, Student Book*

• *Using Language Well, Book 1, Teacher Guide and Answer Key*

Math: Work on your selected math curriculum for about 30 minutes.

Spelling and English: Complete *Using Language Well, Book 1,* Lesson 100.

Lesson 75

Materials Needed
- Typing course of choice
- SCM science course of choice
- Math course of choice

Typing: Work on your selected typing course for about 15 minutes.

Science: In your SCM science course, complete the second assignment for Week 15.

Math: Work on your selected math curriculum for about 30 minutes.

Lesson 76

Materials Needed
- Math course of choice
- Typing course of choice
- *Journaling a Year in Nature* notebooks (optional)

Math: Work on your selected math curriculum for about 30 minutes.

Typing: Work on your selected typing course for about 15 minutes.

Nature Study: Take the whole family outside for nature study.

Lesson 77

Materials Needed
- Math course of choice
- *Spelling Wisdom, Book 1*
- *Using Language Well, Book 1, Student Book*
- *Using Language Well, Book 1, Teacher Guide and Answer Key*

Math: Work on your selected math curriculum for about 30 minutes.

Spelling and English: Complete *Using Language Well, Book 1,* Lesson 101.

Reminder: Assign your student to write one narration from his history, geography, Bible, or science readings this week. Use Rubric 1.3 from Using Language Well, Book 1, Teacher Guide and Answer Key *to help you evaluate his writing. Continue oral narrations daily.*

Lesson 78

Materials Needed
- SCM science course of choice
- Math course of choice

Science: In your SCM science course, complete the first assignment for Week 16.

Math: Work on your selected math curriculum for about 30 minutes.

Lesson 79

Materials Needed
- Math course of choice
- *Spelling Wisdom, Book 1*
- *Using Language Well, Book 1, Student Book*
- *Using Language Well, Book 1, Teacher Guide and Answer Key*

Math: Work on your selected math curriculum for about 30 minutes.

Spelling and English: Complete *Using Language Well, Book 1,* Lesson 102.

Lesson 80

Materials Needed
- Typing course of choice
- SCM science course of choice
- Math course of choice

Typing: Work on your selected typing course for about 15 minutes.

Science: In your SCM science course, complete the second assignment for Week 16.

Math: Work on your selected math curriculum for about 30 minutes.

Lesson 81

Materials Needed
- Math course of choice
- Typing course of choice
- *Journaling a Year in Nature* notebooks (optional)

Math: Work on your selected math curriculum for about 30 minutes.

Typing: Work on your selected typing course for about 15 minutes.

Nature Study: Take the whole family outside for nature study.

Lesson 82

Materials Needed
- Math course of choice
- *Spelling Wisdom, Book 1*
- *Using Language Well, Book 1, Student Book*
- *Using Language Well, Book 1, Teacher Guide and Answer Key*

Math: Work on your selected math curriculum for about 30 minutes.

Spelling and English: Complete *Using Language Well, Book 1*, Lesson 103.

Reminder: Assign your student to write one narration from his history, geography, Bible, or science readings this week. Use Rubric 1.3 from Using Language Well, Book 1, Teacher Guide and Answer Key *to help you evaluate his writing. Continue oral narrations daily.*

Lesson 83

Materials Needed
- SCM science course of choice
- Math course of choice

Science: In your SCM science course, complete the first assignment for Week 17.

Math: Work on your selected math curriculum for about 30 minutes.

Lesson 84

Materials Needed
- Math course of choice
- *Spelling Wisdom, Book 1*
- *Using Language Well, Book 1, Student Book*
- *Using Language Well, Book 1, Teacher Guide and Answer Key*

Math: Work on your selected math curriculum for about 30 minutes.

Spelling and English: Complete *Using Language Well, Book 1,* Lesson 104.

Lesson 85

Materials Needed
- Typing course of choice
- SCM science course of choice
- Math course of choice

Typing: Work on your selected typing course for about 15 minutes.

Science: In your SCM science course, complete the second assignment for Week 17.

Math: Work on your selected math curriculum for about 30 minutes.

Lesson 86

Materials Needed
- Math course of choice
- Typing course of choice
- *Journaling a Year in Nature* notebooks (optional)

Math: Work on your selected math curriculum for about 30 minutes.

Typing: Work on your selected typing course for about 15 minutes.

Nature Study: Take the whole family outside for nature study.

Lesson 87

Materials Needed
- Math course of choice
- *Spelling Wisdom, Book 1*
- *Using Language Well, Book 1, Student Book*
- *Using Language Well, Book 1, Teacher Guide and Answer Key*

Math: Work on your selected math curriculum for about 30 minutes.

Spelling and English: Complete *Using Language Well, Book 1,* Lesson 105.

Reminder: Assign your student to write one narration from his history, geography, Bible, or science readings this week. Use Rubric 1.3 from Using Language Well, Book 1, Teacher Guide and Answer Key *to help you evaluate his writing. Continue oral narrations daily.*

Lesson 88

Materials Needed
- SCM science course of choice
- Math course of choice

Science: In your SCM science course, complete the first assignment for Week 18.

Math: Work on your selected math curriculum for about 30 minutes.

Tip: Remind your student to record in his Book of Mottoes any meaningful quotations, poetry, excerpts, or Scripture passages from recent readings (if he is interested in that ongoing project).

Lesson 89

Materials Needed
- Math course of choice
- *Spelling Wisdom, Book 1*
- *Using Language Well, Book 1, Student Book*
- *Using Language Well, Book 1, Teacher Guide and Answer Key*

Math: Work on your selected math curriculum for about 30 minutes.

Spelling and English: Complete *Using Language Well, Book 1,* Lesson 106.

Lesson 90

Materials Needed
- Typing course of choice
- SCM science course of choice
- Math course of choice

Typing: Work on your selected typing course for about 15 minutes.

Science: In your SCM science course, complete the second assignment for Week 18.

Math: Work on your selected math curriculum for about 30 minutes.

Lesson 91

Materials Needed
- Math course of choice
- Typing course of choice

Notes

• *Journaling a Year in Nature* notebooks (optional)

Math: Work on your selected math curriculum for about 30 minutes.

Typing: Work on your selected typing course for about 15 minutes.

Nature Study: Take the whole family outside for nature study.

Lesson 92

Materials Needed
• Math course of choice
• *Spelling Wisdom, Book 1*
• *Using Language Well, Book 1, Student Book*
• *Using Language Well, Book 1, Teacher Guide and Answer Key*

Math: Work on your selected math curriculum for about 30 minutes.

Spelling and English: Complete *Using Language Well, Book 1*, Lesson 107.

Reminder: Assign your student to write one narration from his history, geography, Bible, or science readings this week. Use Rubric 1.3 from Using Language Well, Book 1, Teacher Guide and Answer Key *to help you evaluate his writing. Continue oral narrations daily.*

Lesson 93

Materials Needed
• SCM science course of choice
• Math course of choice

Science: In your SCM science course, complete the first assignment for Week 19.

Math: Work on your selected math curriculum for about 30 minutes.

Lesson 94

Materials Needed
• Math course of choice
• *Spelling Wisdom, Book 1*
• *Using Language Well, Book 1, Student Book*
• *Using Language Well, Book 1, Teacher Guide and Answer Key*

Math: Work on your selected math curriculum for about 30 minutes.

Spelling and English: Complete *Using Language Well, Book 1*, Lesson 108.

Lesson 95

Materials Needed
- Typing course of choice
- SCM science course of choice
- Math course of choice

Typing: Work on your selected typing course for about 15 minutes.

Science: In your SCM science course, complete the second assignment for Week 19.

Math: Work on your selected math curriculum for about 30 minutes.

Lesson 96

Materials Needed
- Math course of choice
- Typing course of choice
- *Journaling a Year in Nature* notebooks (optional)

Math: Work on your selected math curriculum for about 30 minutes.

Typing: Work on your selected typing course for about 15 minutes.

Nature Study: Take the whole family outside for nature study.

Lesson 97

Materials Needed
- Math course of choice
- *Spelling Wisdom, Book 1*
- *Using Language Well, Book 1, Student Book*
- *Using Language Well, Book 1, Teacher Guide and Answer Key*

Math: Work on your selected math curriculum for about 30 minutes.

Spelling and English: Complete *Using Language Well, Book 1,* Lesson 109.

Reminder: Assign your student to write one narration from his history, geography, Bible, or science readings this week. Use Rubric 1.3 from Using Language Well, Book 1, Teacher Guide and Answer Key *to help you evaluate his writing. Continue oral narrations daily.*

Lesson 98

Materials Needed
- SCM science course of choice
- Math course of choice

Science: In your SCM science course, complete the first assignment for Week 20.

Math: Work on your selected math curriculum for about 30 minutes.

Lesson 99

Materials Needed
- Math course of choice
- *Spelling Wisdom, Book 1*
- *Using Language Well, Book 1, Student Book*
- *Using Language Well, Book 1, Teacher Guide and Answer Key*

Math: Work on your selected math curriculum for about 30 minutes.

Spelling and English: Complete *Using Language Well, Book 1,* Lesson 110.

Lesson 100

Materials Needed
- Typing course of choice
- SCM science course of choice
- Math course of choice

Typing: Work on your selected typing course for about 15 minutes.

Science: In your SCM science course, complete the second assignment for Week 20.

Math: Work on your selected math curriculum for about 30 minutes.

Lesson 101

Materials Needed
- Math course of choice
- Typing course of choice
- *Journaling a Year in Nature* notebooks (optional)

Math: Work on your selected math curriculum for about 30 minutes.

Typing: Work on your selected typing course for about 15 minutes.

Nature Study: Take the whole family outside for nature study.

Lesson 102

Materials Needed
- Math course of choice
- *Spelling Wisdom, Book 1*
- *Using Language Well, Book 1, Student Book*
- *Using Language Well, Book 1, Teacher Guide and Answer Key*

Math: Work on your selected math curriculum for about 30 minutes.

Spelling and English: Complete *Using Language Well, Book 1,* Lesson 111.

Reminder: Assign your student to write one narration from his history, geography, Bible, or science readings this week. Use Rubric 1.3 from Using Language Well, Book 1, Teacher Guide and Answer Key *to help you evaluate his writing. Continue oral narrations daily.*

Lesson 103

Materials Needed
- SCM science course of choice
- Math course of choice

Science: In your SCM science course, complete the first assignment for Week 21.

Math: Work on your selected math curriculum for about 30 minutes.

Tip: Remind your student to record in his Book of Mottoes any meaningful quotations, poetry, excerpts, or Scripture passages from recent readings (if he is interested in that ongoing project).

Lesson 104

Materials Needed
- Math course of choice
- *Spelling Wisdom, Book 1*
- *Using Language Well, Book 1, Student Book*
- *Using Language Well, Book 1, Teacher Guide and Answer Key*

Math: Work on your selected math curriculum for about 30 minutes.

Spelling and English: Complete *Using Language Well, Book 1,* Lesson 112.

Lesson 105

Materials Needed
- Typing course of choice
- SCM science course of choice
- Math course of choice

Typing: Work on your selected typing course for about 15 minutes.

Science: In your SCM science course, complete the second assignment for Week 21.

Math: Work on your selected math curriculum for about 30 minutes.

Lesson 106

Materials Needed
- Math course of choice
- Typing course of choice
- *Journaling a Year in Nature* notebooks (optional)

Math: Work on your selected math curriculum for about 30 minutes.

Typing: Work on your selected typing course for about 15 minutes.

Nature Study: Take the whole family outside for nature study.

Lesson 107

Materials Needed
- Math course of choice
- *Spelling Wisdom, Book 1*
- *Using Language Well, Book 1, Student Book*
- *Using Language Well, Book 1, Teacher Guide and Answer Key*

Math: Work on your selected math curriculum for about 30 minutes.

Spelling and English: Complete *Using Language Well, Book 1,* Lesson 113.

Reminder: Assign your student to write one narration from his history, geography, Bible, or science readings this week. Use Rubric 1.3 from Using Language Well, Book 1, Teacher Guide and Answer Key *to help you evaluate his writing. Continue oral narrations daily.*

Lesson 108

Materials Needed
- SCM science course of choice
- Math course of choice

Science: In your SCM science course, complete the first assignment for Week 22.

Math: Work on your selected math curriculum for about 30 minutes.

Lesson 109

Materials Needed
- Math course of choice
- *Spelling Wisdom, Book 1*
- *Using Language Well, Book 1, Student Book*
- *Using Language Well, Book 1, Teacher Guide and Answer Key*

Math: Work on your selected math curriculum for about 30 minutes.

Spelling and English: Complete *Using Language Well, Book 1*, Lesson 114.

Lesson 110

Materials Needed
- Typing course of choice
- SCM science course of choice
- Math course of choice

Typing: Work on your selected typing course for about 15 minutes.

Science: In your SCM science course, complete the second assignment for Week 22.

Math: Work on your selected math curriculum for about 30 minutes.

Lesson 111

Materials Needed
- Math course of choice
- Typing course of choice
- *Journaling a Year in Nature* notebooks (optional)

Math: Work on your selected math curriculum for about 30 minutes.

Typing: Work on your selected typing course for about 15 minutes.

Nature Study: Take the whole family outside for nature study.

Notes

Lesson 112

Materials Needed
- Math course of choice
- *Spelling Wisdom, Book 1*
- *Using Language Well, Book 1, Student Book*
- *Using Language Well, Book 1, Teacher Guide and Answer Key*

Math: Work on your selected math curriculum for about 30 minutes.

Spelling and English: Complete *Using Language Well, Book 1,* Lesson 115.

Reminder: Assign your student to write one narration from his history, geography, Bible, or science readings this week. Use Rubric 1.3 from Using Language Well, Book 1, Teacher Guide and Answer Key *to help you evaluate his writing. Continue oral narrations daily.*

Lesson 113

Materials Needed
- SCM science course of choice
- Math course of choice

Science: In your SCM science course, complete the first assignment for Week 23.

Math: Work on your selected math curriculum for about 30 minutes.

Lesson 114

Materials Needed
- Math course of choice
- *Spelling Wisdom, Book 1*
- *Using Language Well, Book 1, Student Book*
- *Using Language Well, Book 1, Teacher Guide and Answer Key*

Math: Work on your selected math curriculum for about 30 minutes.

Spelling and English: Complete *Using Language Well, Book 1,* Lesson 116.

Lesson 115

Materials Needed
- Typing course of choice
- SCM science course of choice
- Math course of choice

Typing: Work on your selected typing course for about 15 minutes.

Science: In your SCM science course, complete the second assignment for Week 23.

Math: Work on your selected math curriculum for about 30 minutes.

Lesson 116

Materials Needed
- Math course of choice
- Typing course of choice
- *Journaling a Year in Nature* notebooks (optional)

Math: Work on your selected math curriculum for about 30 minutes.

Typing: Work on your selected typing course for about 15 minutes.

Nature Study: Take the whole family outside for nature study.

Lesson 117

Materials Needed
- Math course of choice
- *Spelling Wisdom, Book 1*
- *Using Language Well, Book 1, Student Book*
- *Using Language Well, Book 1, Teacher Guide and Answer Key*

Math: Work on your selected math curriculum for about 30 minutes.

Spelling and English: Complete *Using Language Well, Book 1,* Lesson 117.

Reminder: Assign your student to write one narration from his history, geography, Bible, or science readings this week. Begin using Rubric 1.4 from Using Language Well, Book 1, Teacher Guide and Answer Key *to help you evaluate his writing. Continue oral narrations daily.*

Lesson 118

Materials Needed
- SCM science course of choice
- Math course of choice

Science: In your SCM science course, complete the first assignment for Week 24.

Math: Work on your selected math curriculum for about 30 minutes.

Tip: Remind your student to record in his Book of Mottoes any meaningful quotations, poetry, excerpts, or Scripture passages from recent readings (if he is interested in that ongoing project).

Lesson 119

Materials Needed
- Math course of choice
- *Spelling Wisdom, Book 1*
- *Using Language Well, Book 1, Student Book*
- *Using Language Well, Book 1, Teacher Guide and Answer Key*

Math: Work on your selected math curriculum for about 30 minutes.

Spelling and English: Complete *Using Language Well, Book 1,* Lesson 118.

Lesson 120

Materials Needed
- Typing course of choice
- SCM science course of choice
- Math course of choice

Typing: Work on your selected typing course for about 15 minutes.

Science: In your SCM science course, complete the second assignment for Week 24.

Math: Work on your selected math curriculum for about 30 minutes.

Term 3

(12 weeks; 5 lessons/week)

Term 3 Resources List

- *Spelling Wisdom, Book 1*
- *Using Language Well, Book 1, Student Book*
- *Using Language Well, Book 1, Teacher Guide and Answer Key*
- Simply Charlotte Mason (SCM) science course of choice
- *Journaling a Year in Nature* notebooks (optional)
- Typing course of choice
- Math course of choice

Weekly Schedule

Day One	Day Two	Day Three	Day Four	Day Five
Math (20–30 min.)	Math (20–30 min.)	Math (20–30 min.)	Math (20–30 min.)	Math (20–30 min.)
	Science (20 min.)		(Nature Study)	Science (20 min.)
Spelling Wisdom & Using Language Well (15 min.)		Typing (10–15 min.)	Spelling Wisdom & Using Language Well (15 min.)	Typing (10–15 min.)

Lesson 121

Materials Needed
- Math course of choice
- *Spelling Wisdom, Book 1*
- *Using Language Well, Book 1, Student Book*
- *Using Language Well, Book 1, Teacher Guide and Answer Key*

Math: Work on your selected math curriculum for about 30 minutes.

Spelling and English: Complete *Using Language Well, Book 1,* Lesson 119.

Reminder: Assign your student to write one narration from his history, geography, Bible, or science readings this week. Use Rubric 1.4 from Using Language Well, Book 1, Teacher Guide and Answer Key *to help you evaluate his writing. Continue oral narrations daily.*

Lesson 122

Materials Needed
- SCM science course of choice
- Math course of choice

Science: In your SCM science course, complete the first assignment for Week 25.

Math: Work on your selected math curriculum for about 30 minutes.

Lesson 123

Materials Needed
- Math course of choice
- Typing course of choice

Math: Work on your selected math curriculum for about 30 minutes.

Typing: Work on your selected typing course for about 15 minutes.

Lesson 124

Materials Needed
- Math course of choice
- *Spelling Wisdom, Book 1*
- *Using Language Well, Book 1, Student Book*
- *Using Language Well, Book 1, Teacher Guide and Answer Key*
- *Journaling a Year in Nature* notebooks (optional)

Math: Work on your selected math curriculum for about 30 minutes.

Spelling and English: Complete *Using Language Well, Book 1,* Lesson 120.

Nature Study: Take the whole family outside for nature study.

Lesson 125

Materials Needed
- Typing course of choice
- SCM science course of choice
- Math course of choice

Typing: Work on your selected typing course for about 15 minutes.

Science: In your SCM science course, complete the second assignment for Week 25.

Math: Work on your selected math curriculum for about 30 minutes.

Lesson 126

Materials Needed
- Math course of choice
- *Spelling Wisdom, Book 1*
- *Using Language Well, Book 1, Student Book*
- *Using Language Well, Book 1, Teacher Guide and Answer Key*

Math: Work on your selected math curriculum for about 30 minutes.

Spelling and English: Complete *Using Language Well, Book 1,* Lesson 121.

Reminder: Assign your student to write one narration from his history, geography, Bible, or science readings this week. Use Rubric 1.4 from Using Language Well, Book 1, Teacher Guide and Answer Key *to help you evaluate his writing. Continue oral narrations daily.*

Lesson 127

Materials Needed
- SCM science course of choice
- Math course of choice

Science: In your SCM science course, complete the first assignment for Week 26.

Math: Work on your selected math curriculum for about 30 minutes.

Lesson 128

Materials Needed
- Math course of choice
- Typing course of choice

Math: Work on your selected math curriculum for about 30 minutes.

Typing: Work on your selected typing course for about 15 minutes.

Lesson 129

Materials Needed
- Math course of choice
- *Spelling Wisdom, Book 1*
- *Using Language Well, Book 1, Student Book*
- *Using Language Well, Book 1, Teacher Guide and Answer Key*
- *Journaling a Year in Nature* notebooks (optional)

Math: Work on your selected math curriculum for about 30 minutes.

Spelling and English: Complete *Using Language Well, Book 1*, Lesson 122.

Nature Study: Take the whole family outside for nature study.

Lesson 130

Materials Needed
- Typing course of choice
- SCM science course of choice
- Math course of choice

Typing: Work on your selected typing course for about 15 minutes.

Science: In your SCM science course, complete the second assignment for Week 26.

Math: Work on your selected math curriculum for about 30 minutes.

Lesson 131

Materials Needed
- Math course of choice
- *Spelling Wisdom, Book 1*
- *Using Language Well, Book 1, Student Book*
- *Using Language Well, Book 1, Teacher Guide and Answer Key*

Math: Work on your selected math curriculum for about 30 minutes.

Notes

Spelling and English: Complete *Using Language Well, Book 1,* Lesson 123.

Reminder: Assign your student to write one narration from his history, geography, Bible, or science readings this week. Begin using Rubric 1.5 from Using Language Well, Book 1, Teacher Guide and Answer Key *to help you evaluate his writing. Continue oral narrations daily.*

Lesson 132

Materials Needed
- SCM science course of choice
- Math course of choice

Science: In your SCM science course, complete the first assignment for Week 27.

Math: Work on your selected math curriculum for about 30 minutes.

Lesson 133

Materials Needed
- Math course of choice
- Typing course of choice

Math: Work on your selected math curriculum for about 30 minutes.

Typing: Work on your selected typing course for about 15 minutes.

Tip: Remind your student to record in his Book of Mottoes any meaningful quotations, poetry, excerpts, or Scripture passages from recent readings (if he is interested in that ongoing project).

Lesson 134

Materials Needed
- Math course of choice
- *Spelling Wisdom, Book 1*
- *Using Language Well, Book 1, Student Book*
- *Using Language Well, Book 1, Teacher Guide and Answer Key*
- *Journaling a Year in Nature* notebooks (optional)

Math: Work on your selected math curriculum for about 30 minutes.

Spelling and English: Complete *Using Language Well, Book 1,* Lesson 124.

Nature Study: Take the whole family outside for nature study.

Lesson 135

Materials Needed
- Typing course of choice
- SCM science course of choice
- Math course of choice

Typing: Work on your selected typing course for about 15 minutes.

Science: In your SCM science course, complete the second assignment for Week 27.

Math: Work on your selected math curriculum for about 30 minutes.

Lesson 136

Materials Needed
- Math course of choice
- *Spelling Wisdom, Book 1*
- *Using Language Well, Book 1, Student Book*
- *Using Language Well, Book 1, Teacher Guide and Answer Key*

Math: Work on your selected math curriculum for about 30 minutes.

Spelling and English: Complete *Using Language Well, Book 1,* Lesson 125.

Reminder: Assign your student to write one narration from his history, geography, Bible, or science readings this week. Use Rubric 1.5 from Using Language Well, Book 1, Teacher Guide and Answer Key *to help you evaluate his writing. Continue oral narrations daily.*

Lesson 137

Materials Needed
- SCM science course of choice
- Math course of choice

Science: In your SCM science course, complete the first assignment for Week 28.

Math: Work on your selected math curriculum for about 30 minutes.

Notes

Lesson 138

Materials Needed
- Math course of choice
- Typing course of choice

Math: Work on your selected math curriculum for about 30 minutes.

Typing: Work on your selected typing course for about 15 minutes.

Lesson 139

Materials Needed
- Math course of choice
- *Spelling Wisdom, Book 1*
- *Using Language Well, Book 1, Student Book*
- *Using Language Well, Book 1, Teacher Guide and Answer Key*
- *Journaling a Year in Nature* notebooks (optional)

Math: Work on your selected math curriculum for about 30 minutes.

Spelling and English: Complete *Using Language Well, Book 1,* Lesson 126.

Nature Study: Take the whole family outside for nature study.

Lesson 140

Materials Needed
- Typing course of choice
- SCM science course of choice
- Math course of choice

Typing: Work on your selected typing course for about 15 minutes.

Science: In your SCM science course, complete the second assignment for Week 28.

Math: Work on your selected math curriculum for about 30 minutes.

Lesson 141

Materials Needed
- Math course of choice
- *Spelling Wisdom, Book 1*
- *Using Language Well, Book 1, Student Book*
- *Using Language Well, Book 1, Teacher Guide and Answer Key*

Math: Work on your selected math curriculum for about 30 minutes.

Spelling and English: Complete *Using Language Well, Book 1*, Lesson 127.

Reminder: Assign your student to write one narration from his history, geography, Bible, or science readings this week. *Use Rubric 1.5 from* Using Language Well, Book 1, Teacher Guide and Answer Key *to help you evaluate his writing. Continue oral narrations daily.*

Lesson 142

Materials Needed
- SCM science course of choice
- Math course of choice

Science: In your SCM science course, complete the first assignment for Week 29.

Math: Work on your selected math curriculum for about 30 minutes.

Lesson 143

Materials Needed
- Math course of choice
- Typing course of choice

Math: Work on your selected math curriculum for about 30 minutes.

Typing: Work on your selected typing course for about 15 minutes.

Lesson 144

Materials Needed
- Math course of choice
- *Spelling Wisdom, Book 1*
- *Using Language Well, Book 1, Student Book*
- *Using Language Well, Book 1, Teacher Guide and Answer Key*
- *Journaling a Year in Nature* notebooks (optional)

Math: Work on your selected math curriculum for about 30 minutes.

Spelling and English: Complete *Using Language Well, Book 1*, Lesson 128.

Nature Study: Take the whole family outside for nature study.

Lesson 145

Materials Needed
- Typing course of choice

Notes

- SCM science course of choice
- Math course of choice

Typing: Work on your selected typing course for about 15 minutes.

Science: In your SCM science course, complete the second assignment for Week 29.

Math: Work on your selected math curriculum for about 30 minutes.

Lesson 146

Materials Needed
- Math course of choice
- *Spelling Wisdom, Book 1*
- *Using Language Well, Book 1, Student Book*
- *Using Language Well, Book 1, Teacher Guide and Answer Key*

Math: Work on your selected math curriculum for about 30 minutes.

Spelling and English: Complete *Using Language Well, Book 1,* Lesson 129.

Reminder: Assign your student to write one narration from his history, geography, Bible, or science readings this week. Use Rubric 1.5 from Using Language Well, Book 1, Teacher Guide and Answer Key *to help you evaluate his writing. Continue oral narrations daily.*

Lesson 147

Materials Needed
- SCM science course of choice
- Math course of choice

Science: In your SCM science course, complete the first assignment for Week 30.

Math: Work on your selected math curriculum for about 30 minutes.

Lesson 148

Materials Needed
- Math course of choice
- Typing course of choice

Math: Work on your selected math curriculum for about 30 minutes.

Typing: Work on your selected typing course for about 15 minutes.

Tip: Remind your student to record in his Book of Mottoes any meaningful quotations, poetry, excerpts, or Scripture passages from recent readings (if he is interested in that ongoing project).

Lesson 149

Materials Needed
- Math course of choice
- *Spelling Wisdom, Book 1*
- *Using Language Well, Book 1, Student Book*
- *Using Language Well, Book 1, Teacher Guide and Answer Key*
- *Journaling a Year in Nature* notebooks (optional)

Math: Work on your selected math curriculum for about 30 minutes.

Spelling and English: Complete *Using Language Well, Book 1,* Lesson 130.

Nature Study: Take the whole family outside for nature study.

Lesson 150

Materials Needed
- Typing course of choice
- SCM science course of choice
- Math course of choice

Typing: Work on your selected typing course for about 15 minutes.

Science: In your SCM science course, complete the second assignment for Week 30.

Math: Work on your selected math curriculum for about 30 minutes.

Lesson 151

Materials Needed
- Math course of choice
- *Spelling Wisdom, Book 1*
- *Using Language Well, Book 1, Student Book*
- *Using Language Well, Book 1, Teacher Guide and Answer Key*

Math: Work on your selected math curriculum for about 30 minutes.

Spelling and English: Complete *Using Language Well, Book 1,* Lesson 131.

Reminder: Assign your student to write one narration from his history, geography, Bible, or science readings this week. Use Rubric 1.5 from Using

Notes

Language Well, Book 1, Teacher Guide and Answer Key *to help you evaluate his writing. Continue oral narrations daily.*

Lesson 152

Materials Needed
- SCM science course of choice
- Math course of choice

Science: In your SCM science course, complete the first assignment for Week 31.

Math: Work on your selected math curriculum for about 30 minutes.

Lesson 153

Materials Needed
- Math course of choice
- Typing course of choice

Math: Work on your selected math curriculum for about 30 minutes.

Typing: Work on your selected typing course for about 15 minutes.

Lesson 154

Materials Needed
- Math course of choice
- *Spelling Wisdom, Book 1*
- *Using Language Well, Book 1, Student Book*
- *Using Language Well, Book 1, Teacher Guide and Answer Key*
- *Journaling a Year in Nature* notebooks (optional)

Math: Work on your selected math curriculum for about 30 minutes.

Spelling and English: Complete *Using Language Well, Book 1,* Lesson 132.

Nature Study: Take the whole family outside for nature study.

Lesson 155

Materials Needed
- Typing course of choice
- SCM science course of choice
- Math course of choice

Typing: Work on your selected typing course for about 15 minutes.

Science: In your SCM science course, complete the second assignment for Week 31.

Math: Work on your selected math curriculum for about 30 minutes.

Lesson 156

Materials Needed
- Math course of choice
- *Spelling Wisdom, Book 1*
- *Using Language Well, Book 1, Student Book*
- *Using Language Well, Book 1, Teacher Guide and Answer Key*

Math: Work on your selected math curriculum for about 30 minutes.

Spelling and English: Complete *Using Language Well, Book 1,* Lesson 133.

Reminder: Assign your student to write one narration from his history, geography, Bible, or science readings this week. Use Rubric 1.5 from Using Language Well, Book 1, Teacher Guide and Answer Key *to help you evaluate his writing. Continue oral narrations daily.*

Lesson 157

Materials Needed
- SCM science course of choice
- Math course of choice

Science: In your SCM science course, complete the first assignment for Week 32.

Math: Work on your selected math curriculum for about 30 minutes.

Lesson 158

Materials Needed
- Math course of choice
- Typing course of choice

Math: Work on your selected math curriculum for about 30 minutes.

Typing: Work on your selected typing course for about 15 minutes.

Lesson 159

Materials Needed
- Math course of choice
- *Spelling Wisdom, Book 1*
- *Using Language Well, Book 1, Student Book*
- *Using Language Well, Book 1, Teacher Guide and Answer Key*
- *Journaling a Year in Nature* notebooks (optional)

Math: Work on your selected math curriculum for about 30 minutes.

Spelling and English: Complete *Using Language Well, Book 1,* Lesson 134.

Nature Study: Take the whole family outside for nature study.

Lesson 160

Materials Needed
- Typing course of choice
- SCM science course of choice
- Math course of choice

Typing: Work on your selected typing course for about 15 minutes.

Science: In your SCM science course, complete the second assignment for Week 32.

Math: Work on your selected math curriculum for about 30 minutes.

Lesson 161

Materials Needed
- Math course of choice
- *Spelling Wisdom, Book 1*
- *Using Language Well, Book 1, Student Book*
- *Using Language Well, Book 1, Teacher Guide and Answer Key*

Math: Work on your selected math curriculum for about 30 minutes.

Spelling and English: Complete *Using Language Well, Book 1,* Lesson 135.

Reminder: Assign your student to write one narration from his history, geography, Bible, or science readings this week. Use Rubric 1.5 from Using Language Well, Book 1, Teacher Guide and Answer Key *to help you evaluate his writing. Continue oral narrations daily.*

Lesson 162

Materials Needed
- SCM science course of choice
- Math course of choice

Science: In your SCM science course, complete the first assignment for Week 33.

Math: Work on your selected math curriculum for about 30 minutes.

Lesson 163

Materials Needed
- Math course of choice
- Typing course of choice

Math: Work on your selected math curriculum for about 30 minutes.

Typing: Work on your selected typing course for about 15 minutes.

Tip: Remind your student to record in his Book of Mottoes any meaningful quotations, poetry, excerpts, or Scripture passages from recent readings (if he is interested in that ongoing project).

Lesson 164

Materials Needed
- Math course of choice
- *Spelling Wisdom, Book 1*
- *Using Language Well, Book 1, Student Book*
- *Using Language Well, Book 1, Teacher Guide and Answer Key*
- *Journaling a Year in Nature* notebooks (optional)

Math: Work on your selected math curriculum for about 30 minutes.

Spelling and English: Complete *Using Language Well, Book 1,* Lesson 136.

Nature Study: Take the whole family outside for nature study.

Lesson 165

Materials Needed
- Typing course of choice
- SCM science course of choice
- Math course of choice

Typing: Work on your selected typing course for about 15 minutes.

Science: In your SCM science course, complete the second assignment for Week 33.

Math: Work on your selected math curriculum for about 30 minutes.

Lesson 166

Materials Needed
- Math course of choice
- *Spelling Wisdom, Book 1*
- *Using Language Well, Book 1, Student Book*
- *Using Language Well, Book 1, Teacher Guide and Answer Key*

Math: Work on your selected math curriculum for about 30 minutes.

Spelling and English: Complete *Using Language Well, Book 1*, Lesson 137.

Reminder: Assign your student to write one narration from his history, geography, Bible, or science readings this week. Use Rubric 1.5 from Using Language Well, Book 1, Teacher Guide and Answer Key *to help you evaluate his writing. Continue oral narrations daily.*

Lesson 167

Materials Needed
- SCM science course of choice
- Math course of choice

Science: In your SCM science course, complete the first assignment for Week 34.

Math: Work on your selected math curriculum for about 30 minutes.

Lesson 168

Materials Needed
- Math course of choice
- Typing course of choice

Math: Work on your selected math curriculum for about 30 minutes.

Typing: Work on your selected typing course for about 15 minutes.

Lesson 169

Materials Needed
- Math course of choice
- *Spelling Wisdom, Book 1*
- *Using Language Well, Book 1, Student Book*
- *Using Language Well, Book 1, Teacher Guide and Answer Key*
- *Journaling a Year in Nature* notebooks (optional)

Math: Work on your selected math curriculum for about 30 minutes.

Spelling and English: Complete *Using Language Well, Book 1,* Lesson 138.

Nature Study: Take the whole family outside for nature study.

Lesson 170

Materials Needed
- Typing course of choice
- SCM science course of choice
- Math course of choice

Typing: Work on your selected typing course for about 15 minutes.

Science: In your SCM science course, complete the second assignment for Week 34.

Math: Work on your selected math curriculum for about 30 minutes.

Lesson 171

Materials Needed
- Math course of choice
- *Spelling Wisdom, Book 1*
- *Using Language Well, Book 1, Student Book*
- *Using Language Well, Book 1, Teacher Guide and Answer Key*

Math: Work on your selected math curriculum for about 30 minutes.

Spelling and English: Complete *Using Language Well, Book 1,* Lesson 139.

Reminder: Assign your student to write one narration from his history, geography, Bible, or science readings this week. Use Rubric 1.5 from Using Language Well, Book 1, Teacher Guide and Answer Key *to help you evaluate his writing. Continue oral narrations daily.*

Lesson 172

Materials Needed
- SCM science course of choice
- Math course of choice

Science: In your SCM science course, complete the first assignment for Week 35.

Math: Work on your selected math curriculum for about 30 minutes.

Lesson 173

Materials Needed
- Math course of choice
- Typing course of choice

Math: Work on your selected math curriculum for about 30 minutes.

Typing: Work on your selected typing course for about 15 minutes.

Lesson 174

Materials Needed
- Math course of choice
- *Spelling Wisdom, Book 1*
- *Using Language Well, Book 1, Student Book*
- *Using Language Well, Book 1, Teacher Guide and Answer Key*
- *Journaling a Year in Nature* notebooks (optional)

Math: Work on your selected math curriculum for about 30 minutes.

Spelling and English: Complete *Using Language Well, Book 1,* Lesson 140.

Nature Study: Take the whole family outside for nature study.

Lesson 175

Materials Needed
- Typing course of choice
- SCM science course of choice
- Math course of choice

Typing: Work on your selected typing course for about 15 minutes.

Science: In your SCM science course, complete the second assignment for Week 35.

Math: Work on your selected math curriculum for about 30 minutes.

Lesson 176

Materials Needed
- Math course of choice
- *Spelling Wisdom, Book 1,* if needed
- *Using Language Well, Book 1, Student Book,* if needed
- *Using Language Well, Book 1, Teacher Guide and Answer Key,* if needed

Math: Work on your selected math curriculum for about 30 minutes.

Spelling and English: Use today and Lesson 179 to catch up on any assignments in *Using Language Well, Book 1,* as needed.

Reminder: Assign your student to write one narration from his history, geography, Bible, or science readings this week. Use Rubric 1.5 from Using Language Well, Book 1, Teacher Guide and Answer Key *to help you evaluate his writing. Continue oral narrations daily.*

Lesson 177

Materials Needed
- SCM science course of choice
- Math course of choice

Science: In your SCM science course, complete the first assignment for Week 36.

Math: Work on your selected math curriculum for about 30 minutes.

Lesson 178

Materials Needed
- Math course of choice
- Typing course of choice

Math: Work on your selected math curriculum for about 30 minutes.

Typing: Work on your selected typing course for about 15 minutes.

Tip: Remind your student to record in his Book of Mottoes any meaningful quotations, poetry, excerpts, or Scripture passages from recent readings (if he is interested in that ongoing project).

Lesson 179

Materials Needed
- Math course of choice
- *Spelling Wisdom, Book 1,* if needed
- *Using Language Well, Book 1, Student Book,* if needed
- *Using Language Well, Book 1, Teacher Guide and Answer Key,* if needed
- *Journaling a Year in Nature* notebooks (optional)

Math: Work on your selected math curriculum for about 30 minutes.

Spelling and English: Use today to catch up on any assignments in *Using Language Well, Book 1,* as needed.

Nature Study: Take the whole family outside for nature study.

Lesson 180

Materials Needed
- Typing course of choice
- SCM science course of choice
- Math course of choice

Typing: Work on your selected typing course for about 15 minutes.

Science: In your SCM science course, complete the second assignment for Week 36.

Math: Work on your selected math curriculum for about 30 minutes.